Stations
& Resurrection
with the Saints

by J. B. Midgley

All booklets are published thanks to the generous support of the members of the Catholic Truth Society

CATHOLIC TRUTH SOCIETY
PUBLISHERS TO THE HOLY SEE

Contents

———

The Lord crushed Him with suffering. If He offers His life in atonement, He shall see His heirs, He shall have a long life and, through Him, all that the Lord wishes will be accomplished. (*Is* 53:10-11)

Let him kiss me with the kisses of his mouth Your love is sweeter than wine

Delicate is the fragrance of your perfume Your name is oil poured out

That is why the maidens love you. (*Sg* 1:2-3)

THE STATIONS

The devotion of 'praying the stations' is treasured by the Church because it preserves a living memory of the words and actions of her Spouse and Lord during His last days on earth, and is a figure of their pilgrimage from earthly exile to their true home in heaven. It expresses the wish of Our Lord's disciples to be conformed to His Passion, and to follow Him as they carry their own daily crosses.

Like the Via Crucis in Jerusalem, the Stations of the Cross may conclude with a commemoration of Our Lord's Resurrection that leaves the faithful with a sense of joyous expectation. To this end, this booklet includes the more recent and increasingly popular Stations of the Resurrection, which invite us to meditate deeply on the words and actions of Jesus from his Resurrection to Pentecost.

By taking to heart sayings and prayers of the saints and others who have gone before us, this devotion, whether in private or public, may be all the richer.

John Paul II - via crucis

Through the weakness of a humiliated and despised man, God manifested his omnipotence. Jesus, the Innocent One, by freely accepting to go to the extreme of obedience to his Father who had sent him, became the witness of God's boundless love for all humanity. The mystery of our salvation is accomplished in the silence of Good Friday when a man, abandoned by all, bearing the weight of our sufferings, was delivered up to death on a Cross, his arms wide open in the gesture of embracing every man and woman. Could greater love be shown? A mystery that is difficult to grasp, a mystery of infinite love! A mystery that inaugurates the new and transfigured world of the Kingdom. On this cross, death has been overcome; from the death of the Son of God made man, life has sprung. His fidelity to the Father's divine plan of love has not been in vain, it has led to the resurrection.

Benedict XVI - *via lucis*

Christ's Resurrection...if we may borrow the language of the theory of evolution,...is the greatest "mutation"; absolutely the most crucial leap into a totally new dimension that there has ever been in the long history of life and its development: a leap into a completely new order which does concern us...What does it mean for us, for the whole world and for me personally? Above all: what happened? Jesus is no longer in the tomb. He is in a totally new life. But how could this happen? What forces were in operation?... His death was an act of love. It is clear that this event...is a qualitative leap in the history of "evolution"... How can this event effectively reach me and draw my life upwards towards itself? The answer, perhaps surprising at first but totally real, is: this event comes to me through faith and Baptism.

Via Crucis

–

The Way of the Cross

Opening Prayer

Lord, you were condemned to death because fear of what others may think suppressed the voice of conscience. How many times have we ourselves preferred success to the truth, our reputation to justice? Strengthen the quiet voice of our conscience that is your own voice in our lives. Let your gaze penetrate our hearts and indicate the direction our lives must take. (*Benedict XVI*)

O Jesus Christ my Lord, with what great love did you Passover the painful road which led you to death; and I, how often have I abandoned you! (*St Alphonsus*)

1. Jesus is condemned to death

V. We adore you Lord and praise you

R. Because by your death and resurrection
you give life to the world

Reading from Holy Scripture

Pilate asked 'What charge do you bring against this man?' They replied, 'If He were not a criminal, we would not be handing Him over to you.'... Pilate brought Jesus out, and seated himself on the chair of judgement about the sixth hour. 'Here is your king,' he said. The chief priests answered, 'We have no king except Caesar.' Pilate ordered him to be scourged, and then handed Him over to them to be crucified (*Mt* 26:3-4; *Jn* 19:12-16).

St Ephraem

Glory to you O Merciful Lord and friend of us all who comes to save us and take away all our sins; who became flesh in the womb of the Virgin, bound in cords, whipped and scourged, mocked and derided, nailed to the Cross; who was buried and rose from the dead.

St Hildegarde

The Creator and Lord of all so loved the world that He sent His Son for our Salvation. The Prince and Saviour of the faithful washed and dried our wounds and gave us the sweetest Medicine, His own Body and Blood, from which all the good things of salvation flow.

St Josemaria Escrivá

Lord, where are your friends?... They have left you. This running away has been going on for twenty centuries... We, all of us, flee from the Cross, from your Holy Cross.

St Padre Pio

Your soul goes in search of a drop of human compassion but alas, you are left alone beneath the weight of indifference.

Dietrich Bonhoeffer

This is what delivering up Jesus means, no longer to take His part, to surrender Him to mockery and the power of the public.

Jerzy Popieluszko

Which side will you take? The side of good or the side of evil? Truth or falsehood? Love or hatred?

Prayer

Lord, those sins of mine were the voices that cried out, 'Let Him be crucified.' The willingness with which I committed them was the consent Pilate gave to the multitude, and my hardness of heart and love of sin were the blows and blasphemies rained on you by the soldiers and the people carrying out the sentence Pilate pronounced. (*John Henry Newman*)

Our Father, Hail Mary, Glory be to the Father.
V. Have mercy on us O Lord. R. Have mercy on us.
May the souls of the faithful departed, through the mercy of God, rest in peace. Amen.

2. Jesus takes up His Cross

V. We adore you Lord and praise you

R. Because by your death and resurrection you
give life to the world

Reading from Holy Scripture

The soldiers led Jesus away to the Praetorium... They
dressed Him in purple, twisted some thorns into a crown
and put it on Him. They saluted Him, 'Hail king of the Jews',
struck His head with a reed, spat on Him, and went down on
their knees to do Him homage. When they had finished, they
took off the purple, and dressed Him in His own clothes. The
soldiers led Him out to crucify Him. Carrying His own cross,
He went out of the city to the place of the skull called
Golgotha. (*Mk* 15:16-20; *Jn* 19:1-3. *Jn* 19:17)

St Elizabeth of Hungary

Here before my eyes is my God and my King; the mild and
merciful Jesus crowned with sharp thorns. Shall I, lowly
creature that I am, remain before Him crowned with gold,
and mock His crown with mine.

St John Baptist De La Salle

Always cling to the Cross of Jesus Christ and never separate
yourself from it. In the face of all the threats of the devil,
boldly say that you will never leave it, nor will anything ever
separate you from it.

St Therese of Lisieux

Suffering is the very best gift Our Lord has to give us. He gives it only to His chosen friends.

St Catherine of Siena

Our Lord says, 'The more perfectly you abandon yourself and resign yourself to me, the more I will console you with my grace and make you feel my presence. But you will never reach the measure of perfection except by a firm, constant, and absolute denial of self-will.

St Padre Pio

Jesus wants you to resemble himself in the torments he endured in the desert, in the Garden and on the Cross... As He toils painfully up the slope of Golgatha we should see Him followed by an immense throng of souls carrying their own crosses and treading the same path.

Prayer

Lord, you willingly subjected yourself to mockery and scorn. Help us so that we never ally ourselves with those who look down on the weak and suffering. Help us to see your face in the lowly and the outcast... Help us to take up the Cross and not to shun it, and may we never complain or become discouraged by life's trials. (*Benedict XVI*)

Our Father, Hail Mary, Glory be to the Father etc.

3. Jesus falls the first time

V. We adore you Lord and praise you

R. Because by your death and resurrection you
give life to the world

Reading from Holy Scripture

For my part, I made no resistance, neither did I turn away. I offered my back to those who struck me, my cheeks to those who tore at my beard. I did not cover my face against insult and spittle... Ours were the sufferings He bore, ours the sorrows He carried, and He was crushed for our sins. On Him lies a punishment that brings us peace, and through His wounds we are healed. (*Is* 50:5-7; 53:4-6)

Pope St Clement I

Let us fix out thoughts on the blood of Christ and reflect how precious that blood is in God's eyes. Its outpouring for our salvation has opened the grace of repentance to those who are willing to turn to Him.

St Teresa Benedicta of the Cross

The burden of the cross that Christ assumed is that of corrupted human nature, with all its consequences in sin and suffering... Christ's fall under the burden of the cross corresponds to the triple fall of humanity: Original Sin; the rejection by His chosen people; the falling away of Christians

John Paul II

Christ does not explain in the abstract the reasons for suffering, but before all else he says: "Follow me!". Come! Take part through your suffering in this work of saving the world, a salvation achieved through my suffering! Through my Cross.

Blessed Charles de Foucauld

The Church is made more perfect by the new crosses You lay upon it every day and the victories it wins daily against the Prince of this world.

Benedict XVI

In Our Lord's fall beneath the weight of His Cross, the meaning of His whole life is seen: His voluntary abasement which lifts us up from the depths of our arrogance that makes us want to be liberated from God and think we do not need His eternal love. Let us allow Our Lord to lift us up by His own abasement, and learn from Him to strip away our illusion of self-sufficiency and independence.

Prayer

My Jesus, it is not the weight of the Cross but of my sins, that has made you suffer so much pain. By the merits of this first fall, deliver me from the misfortune of falling into mortal sin. I repent with my whole heart of having offended you. Never permit me to separate from you again. (*St Alphonsus*)

Our Father, Hail Mary, Glory be to the Father etc.

4. Jesus meets His Mother

V. We adore you Lord and praise you

R. Because by your death and resurrection you
give life to the world

Reading from Holy Scripture

As the Child's father and mother stood there wondering at the things that were being said about Him, Simeon blessed them and said to Mary His Mother, 'You see this Child: He is destined for the fall and the rising of many in Israel, destined to be a sign that is rejected - and a sword will pierce your own soul too - so that the secret thoughts of many will be laid bare. (*Lk* 2:33-335)

God wanted all perfection to be found in Him and all things to be reconciled through Him and for Him, everything in Heaven and everything on earth, when He made peace by His death on the Cross. (*Col* 1:19-20)

St Bernard

The martyrdom of the Virgin Mary, implicit in Simeon's prophecy, is put before us in the story of Our Lord's Passion. Blessed Mother, a sword did pierce your soul, for no sword could penetrate your Son's flesh without piercing your soul. Though he belongs to us all, He was yours in a special sense, and we rightly speak of you as more than a martyr, for the anguish of mind you suffered exceeded all bodily pain.

St Alphonsus

Consider the meeting of the Son and the Mother which took place on this journey. Their looks became like so many arrows to wound those hearts which love each other so tenderly.

Benedict XVI

When Mary heard Simeon's words, she recalled what the prophet Isaiah had said: 'Harshly dealt with, He bore it humbly, He never opened His mouth, like a lamb that is led to the slaughter-house, like a sheep that is dumb before its shearers never opening its mouth.' (*Is* 53:7)

John Paul II

Suffering is an invitation to be more like the Son in doing the Father's will. It offers us an opportunity to imitate Christ who died to redeem mankind from sin. Thus the Father has disposed that suffering can enrich the individual and the whole Church.

Prayer

Lord, it was your will that Mary suffered with her Son in her heart. Grant that, in union with her, the Church may share in the Passion of Christ, and so be brought to the glory of His Resurrection. (*Feast of Our Lady of Sorrows*)

Our Father, Hail Mary, Glory be to the Father etc.

5. Simon of Cyrene helps Jesus to carry the Cross

V. We adore you Lord and praise you

R. Because by your death and resurrection you
give life to the world

Reading from Holy Scripture

If anyone wants to be a follower of mine, let him renounce himself and take up his cross and follow me... They enlisted a passer-by, Simon of Cyrene, father of Alexander and Rufus, who was coming in from the country, to carry his cross. (*Mt* 16:24; *Mk* 15:21)

Diaries of Egeria (4th Century pilgrim to Jerusalem)

As Our Lord staggered up the rocky path to Calvary, the savage treatment He had received was taking its toll. The execution detail commissioned Simon, a Passover pilgrim from Cyrene in North Africa, to help Him carry the cross because they did not want the embarrassment of His dying on the way. Simon, at first reluctant, was moved by the sight of the Saviour's suffering, and this chosen soul willingly shouldered the burden.

Thomas a Kempis

Suffer with Christ and for Christ if you desire to reign with Christ... Jesus now has many lovers of His heavenly Kingdom, but few bearers of His Cross. If you cannot bear joyfully, at least bear patiently; if you bear your cross cheerfully, it will bear you.

St Philip Neri

Bear the Cross and do not make the Cross bear you.

St Katharine Drexel

I adore my Saviour who is crucified, dies on Calvary and is buried in a tomb. I adore the Sacred Heart who desires me to unite myself to His sufferings. I adore the Sacrament that Our Lord instituted to be forever the memorial of His death.

St John Baptist De La Salle

Keep in you heart a sorrow for your sins in union with Our Lord who lived a life of perpetual sacrifice with a heart truly contrite for the sins of the world.

John Paul II

The suffering Christ still dwells among the men and women of today. In order to reveal his power, God has come to share our deepest misery. In every person who is afflicted, beaten, mistreated, rejected, we can discover the Lord who travels the paths of humanity bearing his cross.

Prayer

With Mary, Mother of Christ, we pause beside all the crosses of people today. We ask all the Saints who share Our Lord's suffering in a special way to support us, and we ask all who suffer to become a source of strength for the Church and humanity. (*John Paul II*)

Our Father, Hail Mary, Glory be to the Father etc.

6. Veronica wipes the face of Jesus

V. We adore you Lord and praise you

R. Because by your death and resurrection you
give life to the world

Reading from Holy Scripture

Large numbers of people followed him, and of women
too, who mourned and lamented for him... Anyone who
wants to become great among you must become the servant
to all. The son of man did not come to be served but to
serve, and to give His life as a ransom for many. (*Lk* 23:27;
Mk 10:44-45)

Without beauty, without majesty we saw Him, no looks to
attract our eyes; a thing despised and rejected by men, a man
of sorrows and familiar with suffering, a man to make
people screen their faces; He was despised and we took no
account of Him. (*Is* 53:2-3)

The 'Talmud' (collection of Jewish laws and traditions)

The charitable noblewomen of Jerusalem used to give
soothing drinks to criminals on their way to execution. That
one would certainly have tried to alleviate Jesus' dreadful
condition by some small help, accounts for the tradition that a
brave woman took pity on Him and wiped His face with a
towel on which He left the image of His Face. There were

courageous women disciples who followed Him to the end, and it was natural that one of them should come to His aid. In the East, she has always been honoured as Berenice and, since Roman usage can interchange B and V, Berenice could be Verenice', the holy woman remembered as Veronica.

John Paul II

Dear friends, the Crucified One is ever with you, by the side of those who toil, who suffer, who die. All of you who toil and labour under your burden, come to where Christ dwells, carry your cross with him, present him the offering of your lives, and he will give you rest. At your side, the loving presence of Mary, Mother of Jesus and your mother, will guide you and give you courage and comfort.

Blessed Charles de Foucauld

Let us make Jesus' prayer our own, 'Father, into your hands I commend my spirit.' Father, I abandon myself to you, I entrust myself to you, I put my soul into your hands.

Prayer

Lord, grant us hearts that seek your face. Keep us from the blindness of heart that sees only the surface of things. Impress your face on our hearts so that we encounter you on the way and show your image to the world." (*Benedict XVI*)

Our Father, Hail Mary, Glory be to the Father etc.

7. Jesus falls the second time

V. We adore you Lord and praise you

R. Because by your death and resurrection you
give life to the world

Reading from Holy Scripture

I am the Man familiar with misery under the rod of his
anger. I am the One he has driven and forced to walk in
darkness and without any light. He has blocked my way with
cut stones and obstructed my paths. He has broken my teeth
with gravel and given me ashes for food. (*Lm* 3:1-2, 9, 16)

John Paul II

'Not my will but yours be done'. Our Lord has paid the price
of His obedience to His Father. He has been scourged,
crowned with thorns, and now carries the Cross on the
painful road to his death. He confronts all the temptations
and sins of humanity and in His suffering He reveals God's
love and the meaning of humanity.

St Clare of Assisi

Embrace the poor Christ. Look at Him who became
contemptible for you and follow Him. If you suffer with
Him, you shall rejoice with Him. If you die with Him on the
Cross, you shall possess heavenly mansions in the splendour
of the Saints and, in the Book of Life, your name will be
called glorious.

St John Southworth

When Our Blessed Saviour said, 'He that will be my disciple will take up his cross and follow me,' He practised what He recommended to others. To follow His holy teaching and imitate His holy death, I willingly suffer at present. I look on these gallows as His Cross which I gladly lift up to follow my dear Saviour.

St Ignatius of Loyola

This is the gift proper to the Passion - sorrow in company with Christ in His sorrow, being crushed with the pain that crushed Christ.

John Paul II

The risen Jesus...knows what it is to suffer; he experienced the anguish of death, but by his death he destroyed death itself and is absolutely the first human being to have freed himself from its chains once and for all. He traveled man's whole journey to the heavenly homeland, where he has prepared a throne of glory for each of us.

Prayer

Lord, you have borne all our burdens and you continue to carry us. Our wight made you fall. Lift us up, for by ourselves we cannot rise from the dust. Help us to see the spiritual and material needs of others, and to give them the help they need. Lift us up so that we may lift others up. (*Benedict XVI*)

Our Father, Hail Mary, Glory be to the Father etc.

8. The women of Jerusalem weep for Our Lord

V. We adore you Lord and praise you

R. Because by your death and resurrection you
   give life to the world

Reading from Holy Scripture

The women who had followed Him mourned and lamented for Him, but Jesus turned to them and said, 'Daughters of Jerusalem, do not weep for me; weep rather for yourselves and for your children. The days will surely come when people will say, 'Happy are those who are barren, the wombs that have never borne, the breasts that have never suckled. Then they will begin to say to the mountains, 'Fall on us!'; to the hills, 'Cover us!' For if men use the greenwood like this, what will happen when it is dry? (*Lk* 23:27-32)

The Lord crushed Him with suffering. If He offers His life in atonement, He shall see His heirs, He shall have a long life and, through Him, all that the Lord wishes will be accomplished. (*Is* 53: 10-11)

St Jerome

He is sorrowful about the eventual ruin of Jerusalem that results from the crime about to be committed. He gives a parable about a man who is so set on lighting a fire that he uses green, damp wood instead of dry sticks. If it seems that divine justice is falling on an innocent person, how will it be when it is the turn of the guilty.

St John Bosco

Jesus treated sinners with a kindness and affection that caused some to be shocked, others to be scandalised, and still others to gain hope in God's mercy.

John Paul II

You will find the crucified Lord in the midst of your sickness and suffering.

St Teresa Benedicta of the Cross

Therefore, the Saviour today looks at us, solemnly probing us, and asks each one of us: Will you remain faithful to the Crucified?

John Paul II

Mary, Mother of Hope, accompany us on our journey! Teach us to proclaim the living God; help us to bear witness to Jesus, the one Saviour; make us kindly towards our neighbours, welcoming the needy, concerned for justice, impassioned builders of a more just world.

Prayer

My Jesus, laden with sorrows. I weep for the offences I have committed against you because of the pains they have deserved, and still more because of the displeasure they have caused you who have loved me so much. It is your love more than the fear of hell which causes me to weep for my sins. (*St Alphonsus*)

Our Father, Hail Mary, Glory be to the Father etc.

9. Jesus falls the third time

V. We adore you Lord and praise you

R. Because by your death and resurrection you
give life to the world

Reading from Holy Scripture

It is good for a man to bear the yoke from his youth onwards, to sit in solitude and silence when the Lord fastens it on him, to put his lips to the dust - there may yet be hope; to offer his cheek to the striker, to be overwhelmed with insults. For the Lord does not reject mankind for ever. If He has punished, He has compassion, so great is His kindness. (*Lm* 3:27-32)

Blessed Angela of Foligno

Inquire and meditate on the Passion and the Cross. Even if you cannot suffer with Our Lord from the heart, at least do it earnestly and carefully with your lips. When something is often said in this way, in the end it imparts warmth to the heart.

St John of Avila

Adam lost the earthly paradise and sought it weeping. Through His love of the Cross, Our Lord gave him another Paradise fairer than the old where shines the light of the Holy Trinity. I pray God may open your eyes and let you see what hidden treasures He bestows on us in the trials from which the world thinks only to flee.

St Alphonsus

Consider Our Lord's third fall. His weakness was extreme, and the cruelty of His executions excessive, who tried to hasten His steps when He could scarcely move.

Blessed Anna Katharine Emmerich (visionary)

It was about a quarter to twelve when Jesus, loaded with His Cross, sank down at the precise point where He was to be crucified. The hearts of the barbarous executioners were harder than iron itself. They measured him and marked the places for His feet and hands.

Benedict XVI

The tradition that Our Lord fell three times beneath the weight of the Cross calls to mind the fall of Adam, the state of fallen humanity and the mystery of Our Lord's sharing in our fall. The Lord bears the burdens of humanity and falls but, in doing so, He meets us, gazes on us and touches our hearts. He falls in order to raise us up.

Prayer

Almighty God, the love you offer, always exceeds the furthest expression of the human heart. Direct each thought, each effort of our life, so that the limits of our faults and weaknesses may not obscure the vision of your glory or keep us from the peace you have promised.

Our Father, Hail Mary, Glory be to the Father etc.

10. Jesus is stripped of His garments and offered gall

V. We adore you Lord and praise you

R. Because by your death and resurrection you give life to the world

Reading from Holy Scripture

When they had reached a place called Golgotha, that is the place of the skull, they gave Him wine to drink mixed with gall which he tasted but refused to drink... The soldiers took His clothing and divided it into four shares, one for each soldier. (*Mt* 27:33-35; *Jn* 19:23-24)

I can count every one of my bones. These people stare at me and gloat; they divide my clothing among them. They cast lots for my robe. (*Ps* 21:18-19)

John Henry Newman

Our Lord has arrived at the place of sacrifice and the soldiers begin to prepare Him for the Cross. His garments are torn from His bleeding Body and He, the Holy of Holies, stands exposed to the gaze of the coarse and scoffing multitude.

Margaret Sinclair

O My Jesus, you accept it with patience and resignation, as you desired our redemption. You think nothing of the suffering it will cost you or your immaculate Mother...

John Paul II

There is no sin which cannot be forgiven, if we approach the throne of mercy with humble and contract hearts.

Blessed Teresa of Calcutta

Christ's passion is being relived everywhere. May we be willing to share people's sufferings throughout the world... he chose poverty because he knew that it was the genuine means to posses God and to bring his love to the earth.

St Padre Pio

Jesus, the Man of Sorrows, wants all Christians to imitate him. Now, Jesus has offered this chalice to me also

Benedict XVI

Our Lord is now an outcast, despised by all alike. The stripping reminds us of the expulsion from Paradise: God's splendour has fallen away from man who now stands naked and shamed. Once more, Our Lord has taken on the condition of fallen man. Stripped of His clothing, He reminds us that we have all lost the "first garment" that is God's splendour.

Prayer

Lord, you were stripped of your garments, took upon yourself the shame of Adam and healed it. You also take to yourself the sufferings and needs of the poor and the outcasts. This is how you make us realize that your Father holds you and all of us in the world in His hands. Clothe us in the light of your grace. (*Benedict XVI*)

Our Father, Hail Mary, Glory be to the Father etc.

11. Jesus is nailed to the Cross

V. We adore you Lord and praise you

R. Because by your death and resurrection you
   give life to the world

Reading from Holy Scripture

They crucified Him there and two robbers, one on the
right, the other on the left... One of the robbers abused
Him: 'Are you not the Christ? Save yourself and us as well.'
The other rebuked him, 'Have you no fear of God at all?
You received the same sentence as He did but in our case we
deserved it. But this man has done nothing wrong. Jesus,' he
said, 'remember me when you come into your Kingdom.'
'Indeed I promise you,' He replied, 'today you will be with
me in Paradise.' (*Mt* 17:37-42; *Lk* 23:33-34)

St Andrew of Crete

Like the Thief, I cry out to you, 'Remember me when you
come into your Kingdom.' Have mercy on me O God, have
mercy on me.

St Ignatius of Antioch

The Eucharist is the flesh of our crucified Saviour. I am
resolved to bear witness to Him in my martyrdom. The
Christians of Smyrna, in their invincible faith, are nailed
with flesh and blood to the Cross of Our Lord Jesus Christ.

St Catherine of Sweden

Our Lord was crucified not in a cathedral but on a Cross between two thieves.

St Claude de la Colombiere

Lord, if I am to complain, let me complain to you fastened upon your Cross. You know my sufferings are far less than I deserve. I come to you so that you will give me the strength to suffer in silence just as you did.

St Vincent de Paul

Now who denies himself and takes up his cross and follows Christ better than he who seeks not to do his own will, but always that of God?

St Francis of Assisi

You together with them have crucified Him and crucify Him even now by delighting in vices and sins.

Prayer

Lord, you let yourself be nailed to the Cross, accepting the terrible cruelty of this suffering, the destruction of your body and your dignity. You allowed yourself to be nailed fast; you did not try to escape or lessen your suffering. May we never flee from what you ask us to do. Help us to remain faithful to you and unmask the false freedom that distances us from you. Help us to accept your binding freedom so that, bound fast to you, we discover true freedom. (*Benedict XVI*)

Our Father, Hail Mary, Glory be to the Father etc.

12. Jesus dies on the Cross

V. We adore you Lord and praise you

R. Because by your death and resurrection you
    give life to the world

Reading from Holy Scripture

Seeing His Mother and the disciple He loved standing near her, He said to His Mother, 'Woman, this is your son.' Then to the disciple he said, 'This is you Mother.' And from that moment the disciple made a place for her in his home... Jesus knew that everything had been accomplished and, to fulfil the scripture perfectly He said, 'I am thirsty.'... After Jesus had taken the vinegar He said, 'It is accomplished; and bowing His head He gave up His spirit to His Father. (*Mt* 27:45-54; *Jn* 19:28-30)

St Bonaventure

God's providence decreed that one of the soldiers should open Our Lord's side with a spear so that blood and water might flow out to pay the price of our salvation. This Blood from the secret recesses of His heart gives the sacrament of the Church the power to confer the life of grace.

St Thomas Aquinas

O soft self-wounding Pelican whose breast weeps balm for wounded man; that blood, whose least drops sovereign be to wash my worlds of sin from me.

St Paul of the Cross

Conceal yourself in Jesus crucified and hope for nothing other than that all His creation will be converted to His will.

St John Eudes

I see many crucified persons in the world but few who are crucified by the love of Jesus. Some are crucified by their self-love and inordinate attachment to the world. Happy are they who are crucified for the love of Jesus, those who live and die on the Cross with Him.

John Paul II

By his dying on the Cross, Christ shows us how to make sense of our suffering. In his Passion we find the inspiration and strength of turn away from any temptation to resentment and grow through pain into new life.

Blessed Teresa of Calcutta

On the cross Christ was deprived of everything. The cross itself had been given Him by Pilate; nails and the crown, by the soldiers. He was naked

Prayer

O most gentle Jesus, you have redeemed us by Baptism from original sin. Now, by your precious Blood offered and received throughout the world, deliver us from all evils, past, present, and to come. By your most bitter death, give us a lively faith, a firm hope, and a perfect charity, so that we may love you with all our hearts. (*St Clare of Assisi*)

Our Father, Hail Mary, Glory be to the Father etc.

13. Jesus is taken down from the Cross and laid in the arms of His Mother

V. We adore you Lord and praise you

R. Because by your death and resurrection you
    give life to the world

Reading from Holy Scripture

And many women were there, watching from a distance,
the same women who had followed Jesus from Galilee
and looked after Him... When it was evening, there came a
rich man, Joseph of Arimathea who had become a disciple of
Jesus. He went to Pilate and asked for His body, and Pilate
ordered it to be handed over. (*Mt* 27:55-58)

St Alphonsus

Consider how, after Our Lord had expired, two of His disciples,
Joseph and Nicodemus, took Him down from the Cross and
laid Him in the arms of His afflicted Mother who received Him
with unutterable tenderness and pressed Him to her bosom.

St Bernard

Mary endured martyrdom in her soul, an anguish of mind
exceeding all bodily pain. Could her Son die bodily and she
not share His death in her heart? It was love that moved Him
to suffer death, and it was love that moved Mary, the like of
which no mother has ever known.

St Thomas More

Give me your grace to long for your Holy Sacraments and rejoice in the presence of your precious Body in the Holy Sacrament of the Altar; and at the high Memorial, with tender compassion to remember your most bitter Passion.

St John of the Cross

If you would understand that the Cross is Our Lord's triumph, hear what he Himself said: 'If I am lifted up, I will draw all people to myself.' In sharing His Cross, you are seeking His glory.

Blessed John XXIII

Mary is still there at the foot of the Cross, as she was beside the Babe at Bethlehem. Let us pray to her, this Mother, so that she too may pray for us 'now and at the hour of our death.'

St Teresa of Avila

Look at what our Spouse's love for us cost Him; in order to free us from death... Fix your eyes on the Crucified and everything will become small for you.

Prayer

Lord, in the hour of darkness, help us know that you are still there. Help us not to leave you alone. Give us the fidelity to withstand moments of desolation and be ready to embrace you in your helplessness, like your Mother who holds you to her breast. (*Benedict XVI*)

Our Father, Hail Mary, Glory be to the Father etc.

14. Jesus is laid in the tomb

V. We adore you Lord and praise you

R. Because by your death and resurrection you
give life to the world

Reading from Holy Scripture

Joseph took the body, wrapped it in a clean shroud and put it in his own new tomb which he had hewn out of rock. He then rolled a large stone across the entrance of the tomb and went away. (*Mt* 27: 57-61)

They gave Him a grave with the wicked; a tomb with the rich though he had done no wrong and there was no perjury in His mouth. (*Is* 53:9)

St Clement of Alexandria

Christ Our Lord has turned all our sunsets into dawn.

St Bonaventure

Crucified we Thee adore; Thee with all our hearts implore: with the Saints our souls unite in the realms of heavenly light.

Blessed John XXIII

Throughout the ages, the faithful have been drawn to a passionate love of Our Lord's Cross, and have offered penance and suffering as their share in His Mystical Body. In the Sacrifice of the Cross, we contemplate the Saints who are the 'oblations and whole burnt-offerings', and whose lives are the glory of the Church. These sacrifices are an image of the Eucharist in which the Sacrifice of the Cross is renewed by the Divine Victim on our altars every day.

St John Fisher

Our Lord offered sacrifice here on earth when He underwent His most bitter death. Then, clothed with the new garment of immortality, He entered the Holy of Holies, that is, He went into heaven.

John Paul II

As a personal act, sin has its first and most important consequences in the sinner himself: that is, in his relationship with God, who is the very foundation of human life; and also in his spirit, weakening his will and clouding his intellect.

Benedict XVI

The Resurrection is a cosmic event, which includes heaven and earth and links them together. In the words of the Exsultet once again, we can proclaim: "Christ...who came back from the dead and shed his peaceful light on all mankind, your Son who lives and reigns for ever and ever". Amen!

Prayer

Father, in your plan of Salvation, your Son Jesus Christ accepted the Cross and freed us from the power of the enemy. May we come to share the glory of His Resurrection, for he lives and reigns forever and ever.

Our Father, Hail Mary, Glory be to the Father etc.

Concluding prayer

Father, the suffering and death of your Son brought life to the world. Though sinless, He accepted death to save the guilty, by dying destroyed our sins, and in His Resurrection, He has raised us up to holiness. You decreed that Man should be saved through the wood of the Cross. Now the tree of Adam's defeat becomes the tree of Our Lord's victory; where life was lost, life has been restored. We praise you Lord with all the angels and the saints.

Via Lucis

–

The Way of the Resurrection

The devotions of Holy Week are directed to the Resurrection which is, as St Paul says, the basis of our Faith. If we are united with Our Lord in His Passion and death, we share in His Resurrection. If we are with Him in His holocaust on Calvary, we accompany Him in His glory. (*St Josemaria Escrivá*)

Opening Prayer

Father we praise you with joy when Christ became our Paschal Sacrifice. By dying, He destroyed our death; by rising, He restored our life.

1. Jesus rises from the dead

V. We adore you Lord and praise you

R. Because by your death and resurrection
   you give life to the world

Reading from Holy Scripture

After the Sabbath, and towards dawn on the first day of the week, Mary of Magdala and the other Mary went to visit the sepulchre. And all at once there was a violent earthquake, for the angel of the Lord, descending from heaven, came and rolled away the stone and sat on it...and he said to the women, 'There is no need for you to be afraid. I know you are looking for Jesus, who was crucified. He is not here, for he has risen, as he said he would... He has risen from the dead and now he is going before you to Galilee; it is there you will see him. (*Mt* 28:1-7)

St John Chrysostom

As Our Lord was born from His Mother's virginal womb, so He rose again from the closed tomb. As the only-begotten Son of God was made the firstborn of His mother so, by His Resurrection, He has become the firstborn from the dead. 'Come, see the place where He lay.' See the place where the signs of our own resurrection are portrayed, where the seed of mortality brings forth a rich harvest of immortality.

St Theodore

How splendid is the Cross of Christ. It brings life, not death,
light not darkness, Paradise, not its loss. It is the wood on
which the Lord, like a great Warrior, was wounded in hands,
feet and side, but thereby He healed our wounds. A tree had
destroyed us, and now a tree has brought us to life.

Blessed John XXIII

Death is challenged and defeated in Our Lord's greatest
victory. The Resurrection is also an assurance of victory for
the Church against all adversities and persecution. 'Christ
conquers! Christ reigns! Christ rules!'

St Padre Pio

After Mass, I remained with Jesus in thanksgiving. How
sweet was the colloquy with Paradise that morning. The
heart of Jesus and my own were fused, no longer two hearts
beating but only one.

Prayer

Dear Lord, you have destroyed death with all its pains
and tears, Grief that gnaws the mind has fled. A sudden
shaft of light from Christ our God bursts forth and now this
mortal world is shining. (*St Methodius*)

Our Father, Hail Mary, Glory be to the Father.
V. Jesus, the Lord, is Risen. R. Alleluia, Alleluia.

2. The disciples find the empty tomb

V. We adore you Lord and praise you

R. Because by your death and resurrection
   you give life to the world

Reading from Holy Scripture

So Peter set out with the other disciple to go to the tomb. They ran together, but the other disciple, running faster than Peter, reached the tomb first; he bent down and saw the linen cloths lying on the ground, but did not go in. Simon Peter who was following now came up, went right into the tomb, saw the linen cloths on the ground, and also the cloth that had been over his head... Then the other disciple who had reached the tomb first also went in; he saw and he believed. Till this moment they had failed to understand the teaching of scripture, that he must rise from the dead. (*Jn* 20:1-9)

St Ignatius of Antioch

We have one Lord, the Doctor active in Body and Soul, Begotten yet Unbegotten, God in man, true Life in death, Son of Mary and Son of God, first able to suffer and now unable to suffer.

St Romanus

Sing hymns to Him, praise Him who suffered and died for us and, when you soon behold Him, welcome Him to your hearts. He has risen from the tomb and makes you new. Prepare a pure heart so that our King will dwell there and make it a Heaven. He will soon come to fill those who suffer with joy, and Adam will rejoice.

St Maximilian Kolbe

The God of Love was not content to redeem me in this terrible, though generous fashion. He remains on this earth in the holiest and most admirable Sacrament of the Altar, and comes to me, unites Himself to me under the appearance of food. His Blood flows in my blood; His soul permeates my soul giving it strength and nourishment. What wonders!

John Paul II

Though not mentioned in the Scriptures, it is conceivable that the Risen Lord appeared first to His Mother Mary, and that she was present with the other Disciples when He ascended into Heaven.

Prayer

Help me to understand that the fruit of Silence is Prayer; the fruit of Prayer is Faith; the fruit of Faith is Love; the Fruit of Love is Service; the fruit of Service is Peace. (*Blessed Teresa of Calcutta*)

Our Father, Hail Mary, Glory be to the Father etc.

3. The risen Lord appears to Mary Magdalen

V. We adore you Lord and praise you

R. Because by your death and resurrection
you give life to the world

Reading from Holy Scripture

Then, still weeping, Mary stooped to look inside, and saw two angels in white sitting where the body of Jesus had been... They said, 'Woman, why are you weeping?' 'They have taken my Lord away' she replied 'and I don't know where they have put him.'... She turned round and saw Jesus standing there, though she did not recognise him. Jesus said, 'Woman, why are you weeping? Who are you looking for?' Supposing him to be the gardener, she said, 'Sir, if you have taken him away, tell me where you have put him, and I will go and remove him'. Jesus said, 'Mary!' She knew him then and said to him in Hebrew, - 'Rabbuni!'- which means Master. (*Jn* 20:11-18)

St Gregory the Great

We reflect upon the ardent love in the heart of this woman who would not leave the Lord's grave even after His other disciples had gone away. She continued seeking Him whom she could not find; in tears she kept searching; and afire with love she yearned for Him whom she thought had been removed. Then she alone saw Him, she who had remained behind to seek Him, because what is good involves perseverance. Truth Himself has said: 'Those who persevere to the end shall be saved.'

St John Chrysostom

Let everyone who loves God, rejoice in the festival of Light; let the faithful servant enter into the joy of the Lord. Those who have fasted must rejoice today; and every one come without misgivings. The table is laid, the fatted calf is saved, let all take their fill. All of you share in the Banquet of faith; all of you draw on the wealth of God's mercy.

St Bernadette

In Holy Communion you must give God a good reception. We have every interest in welcoming Him, and then he has to pay us for His lodging.

Prayer

My God, I choose the whole lot; no point in becoming a saint by halves. I am not afraid of suffering for your sake; the only thing I am afraid of is clinging to my own will. Take it, for I want for myself everything that is your will, no matter what. (*St Therese of Lisieux*)

Our Father, Hail Mary, Glory be to the Father etc.

4. The risen Lord appears to two disciples on the road to Emmaus

V. We adore you Lord and praise you

R. Because by your death and resurrection
   you give life to the world

Reading from Holy Scripture

Two of them were on their way to a village called Emmaus,...and they were talking together about all that had happened. Now as they talked this over, Jesus himself came up and walked by their side; but something prevented them from recognising him. He said to them, 'What matters are you discussing as you walk along?'...'All about Jesus of Nazareth' they answered 'who proved he was a great prophet...and how our chief priests and our leaders handed him over to be sentenced to death... Our own hope had been that he would be the one to set Israel free'. Then he said to them, 'You foolish men! So slow to believe the full message of the prophets! Was it not ordained that the Christ should suffer and so enter into his glory?' (*Lk* 24:13-19, 25-27)

St Jerome

The two disciples were disappointed because they had been hoping for an immediate Messianic reign in Israel. Our lord's Kingdom is not of this world.

St Thomas Aquinas

Approach the Supper of the Lord, the table of plenitude and holiness, then you will come to the Wedding Feast of the Lamb and taste bread in the Kingdom of the Father; and our host shall be Our Lord Jesus Christ whose power and empire are without end.

St John Fisher

Our Lord's eternal Sacrifice is offered every moment of every hour so that we have the strongest possible consolation and support. A share in this holy and eternal sacrifice is given to all who are contrite and resolved not to repeat their faults.

St Gemma Galgani

Behold me at your Most Sacred Feet, dear Jesus, to show every moment my recognition and gratitude for the many and continued favours you have given me, and that you still wish to give me. Whenever I have called to you, O Jesus, you have made me happy; whenever I have had recourse to you, you have consoled me.

Prayer

Lord set my heart on fire with love of your Word and Sacrament. Guide me on the right path that I may see your face in the faces of others, hear your voice in the proclamation of the Word, recognise you in the breaking of Bread, and be a sign of your presence in the world.

Our Father, Hail Mary, Glory be to the Father etc.

5. The risen Lord reveals himself at the breaking of bread

V. We adore you Lord and praise you

R. Because by your death and resurrection
   you give life to the world

Reading from Holy Scripture

When they drew near to the village to which they were going, he made as if to go on; but they pressed him to stay with them. 'It is nearly evening' they said 'and the day is almost over.' So he went in to stay with them. Now while he was with them at table, he took the bread and said the blessing; then he broke it and handed it to them. And their eyes were opened and they recognised him; but he had vanished from their sight. Then they said to each other, 'Did not our hearts burn within us as he talked to us on the road and explained the scriptures to us?' (*Lk* 24:28-35)

St Justin

Their eyes were opened and they knew Him when He broke the bread. When bread is broken, it is, in a way diminished. 'Breaking' helps us understand the virtue of humility by which Our Lord, even He who is the Bread of Life, broke, and emptied Himself, and so gave us knowledge of Himself.

St Augustine

We are given new heart when we see ourselves so much better off than those to whom the Lord appeared as they were walking down the road that day. We believe what they as yet did not believe; they had lost hope, but we have no doubts about those things that caused their uncertainty. It was in the breaking of bread that the Lord wished to be recognized by those who did not realise who He was. As believers, we now know Christ in the breaking not of any kind of bread, but the bread that has been blessed by Christ and has now become His Body.

John Paul II

In the wonderful Sacrament of the Eucharist, the Holy Spirit makes present for us the one, saving Sacrifice of Our Lord's death and Resurrection. Sins are forgiven and new life inherited with the reception of the living Body and Blood of our risen and glorified Lord. Here and now, we experience the work of Redemption, and joyfully look forward to eternal life in the Trinity which the Sacred Victim has won for us.

Prayer

God our Father, the disciples recognised you in the breaking of bread. May this sharing in the sacrament of your Son free us from our old life of sin and make us your new creation.

Our Father, Hail Mary, Glory be to the Father etc.

6. The risen Lord appears to his disciples

V. We adore you Lord and praise you

R. Because by your death and resurrection
   you give life to the world

Reading from Holy Scripture

They were still talking about all this when he himself stood among them and said to them, 'Peace be with you!' In a state of alarm and fright, they thought they were seeing a ghost. But he said, 'Why are you so agitated, and why are these doubts rising in your hearts? Look at my hands and feet; yes, it is I indeed. Touch me and see for yourselves; a ghost has no flesh and bones as you can see I have.' And as he said this he showed them his hands and feet. Their joy was so great that they still could not believe it, and they stood there dumbfounded. (*Lk* 24:36-43)

St Jerome

When Our Lord greeted the disciples, 'Peace be with you!' He meant Himself. The Spirit of Christ fills with every blessing all who share in Him.

St Cyril of Alexandria

By His miraculous entry through closed doors, Our Lord proved to the disciples that by nature He was God, and that he was also none other than the Companion whom they had followed and love. By showing Thomas and the others His side and the marks of the nails, He convinced them that He had raised the Temple of His body that had hung on the Cross. He had destroyed death's power over flesh because, as God, He was life itself.

St Padre Pio

Jesus and your soul must cultivate the vineyard together. It is for you to pick up and carry away the stones, to pull out the thorn bushes. It is the task of Jesus to sow, plant, cultivate and to water.

Benedict XVI

Faith in the Resurrection appreciates God's power and the purpose of human responsibility. God's power is hope and joy in the liberation He reveals at Eastertide. In the Pasch, He shows the power of the Trinity's love that is superior to the power of death, and gives us the right to sing 'Alleluia' in a world otherwise overcast with a cloud of death.

Prayer

Lord, you have convinced me that your beauty, power and perfection are the glory of the highest heavens. If I follow you, you will teach me to know you and reveal your loveliness to me in its eternal splendour. (*St Margaret Mary Alacoque*)

Our Father, Hail Mary, Glory be to the Father etc.

7. The risen Lord gives the power to forgive sins

V. We adore you Lord and praise you

R. Because by your death and resurrection
   you give life to the world

Reading from Holy Scripture

In the evening of that same day…the doors were closed in the room where the disciples were… Jesus came and stood among them. He said to them, 'Peace be with you', and showed them his hands and his side. The disciples were filled with joy when they saw the Lord…'Peace be with you. As the Father sent me, so am I sending you.' After saying this he breathed on them and said: 'Receive the Holy Spirit. For those whose sins you forgive, they are forgiven; for those whose sins you retain, they are retained.' (*Jn* 20:19-23)

St Gregory of Nyssa

Let us consider how God continually reveals to us the Resurrection that is to be. He has made Our Lord the first fruits of this by raising Him from the dead.

St Gregory the Great

The Father sent His Son whom He loved into the world, incarnate for the redemption of the human race. It was His will that he should come into the world to suffer. In the same way, when Our Lord sent the disciples He loves into the world, it is not to enjoy its pleasures; on the contrary, He sent them to face suffering as He Himself had endured.

St Edmund Campion

Christ is rich who will maintain you; He is a King who will provide you; He is a sumptuous entertainer who will feast you; He is beautiful who will give in abundance all that can make you happy. Enrol yourselves in His service.

St Bernadette

My God, it is your will. I accept the cup that you have given me. Blessed be your holy name.

John Paul II

Our Lord first appeared to the disciples in the Upper Room, He revealed to them the power to forgive sins that belongs to God alone. It is through His Passion and redemptive death that the Church, with the power of the Holy Spirit, has been entrusted with this power.

Prayer

Mary our Mother, you are the Handmaid of the Lord. Give us some share in your willingness to serve God and the salvation of the world. Open our hearts to the great anticipation of God's Kingdom and the proclamation of the Gospel to all Creation. (*Blessed John XXIII*).

Our Father, Hail Mary, Glory be to the Father etc.

8. The risen Lord confirms the faith of Thomas

V. We adore you Lord and praise you

R. Because by your death and resurrection
you give life to the world

Reading from Holy Scripture

Thomas…was not with them when Jesus came,…he answered, 'Unless I see the holes that the nails made in his hands and can put my finger into the holes they made, and unless I can put my hand into his side, I refuse to believe'. Eight days later the disciples were in the house again and Thomas was with them. The doors were closed, but Jesus came in and stood among them. 'Peace be with you' he said. Then he spoke to Thomas, 'Put your finger here; look, here are my hands. Give me your hand; put it into my side.' Doubt no longer but believe.' Thomas replied, 'My Lord and my God!' Jesus said to him:' You believe because you can see me. Happy are those who have not seen and yet believe.' (*Jn* 20:24-29)

St Augustine

Our Lord could have risen with a body from which the marks of wounds had been erased, but He knew the disciples had a wound in their hearts so deep that its only cure was to retain the scars of His own wounds. He answered Thomas' confession. 'My Lord and my God' with, 'You believe because you have seen me; blessed are those who have not seen and yet believe.'

St Gregory the Great

Without Thomas' misgivings, we should never have known that Jesus was nailed to the Cross, for he alone in the New Testament mentions nails and the marks they leave. We are more confirmed in our faith by his doubts that by the faith of others, and by his scepticism that becomes a declamation of Our Lord's divinity.

St Bernardino of Siena

Thomas' doubts and subsequent encounter with the Risen Lord strengthened faith and brought a keener insight, and He is the only person in the Gospels who hails Jesus directly as God. He arrived at an understanding of the union of the divine and human natures in the one person of Jesus Christ and, from his incredulity comes the strongest evidence of the Resurrection.

Prayer

Lord, I am not like Thomas. I cannot see your wounds but, like him, I can call you my Lord and my God. In this belief deepen my faith and my hope, and every day increase my love of you. (*St Thomas Aquinas*).

Our Father, Hail Mary, Glory be to the Father etc.

9. The risen Lord meets his disciples on the shore of Galilee

V. We adore you Lord and praise you

R. Because by your death and resurrection
   you give life to the world

Reading from Holy Scripture

It was light by now and there stood Jesus on the shore, though the disciples did not realise that it was Jesus. Jesus called out, 'Have you caught anything, friends?' And when they answered, 'No', he said, 'Throw the net out to starboard and you'll find something'. So they dropped the net, and there were so many fish that they could not haul it in. The disciple Jesus loved said to Peter, 'It is the Lord'... As soon as they came ashore they saw that there was some bread there, and a charcoal fire with fish cooking on it. Jesus then stepped forward, took the bread and gave it to them, and the same with the fish. (*Jn* 21:1-9, 13)

St Jerome

The detail of the number of fish is important because the ancient world believed one hundred and fifty-three to be the exact number of all known species of fish, It indicates the universality of God's love, and the Church who embraces a new people from every corner of the globe.

St Irenaeus

When the disciples came ashore and Jesus cooked them breakfast, it was to assure them that He was no apparition but was physically present, again in the breaking of bread.

St John Baptist De La Salle

The early disciples were accustomed to communicate every day, and the practice was continued in the Church for a very long time. Several Fathers of the Church show how this was in keeping with Our Lord's intention when He instituted the Holy Eucharist, for they apply the words of the Lord's Prayer, 'our daily bread', to the Body of Christ we receive in Holy communion, looking upon it as the Bread with which we should feed our souls every day.

John Paul II

Living word of the Father, stay with us on our journey through history. Give hope and trust to all who search for the meaning of their lives. Bread of Eternal Life, nourish those who hunger for freedom, justice and peace.

Prayer

O eternal Trinity, your divine nature is made precious in the Body and Blood of the only-begotten Son. Fill my soul that it may ever continue to hunger and thirst for you who are the Light. (*St Catherine of Siena*)

Our Father, Hail Mary, Glory be to the Father etc.

10. The risen Lord confers primacy on Peter

V. We adore you Lord and praise you
R. Because by your death and resurrection
you give life to the world

Reading from Holy Scripture

After the meal Jesus said to Simon Peter, 'Simon son of John, do you love me more than these others do?' He answered, 'Yes Lord, you know I love you'. Jesus said to him, 'Feed my lambs'. A second time he said to him, 'Simon son of John, do you love me?' He replied, 'Yes, Lord, you know I love you'. Jesus said to him, 'Look after my sheep'. Then he said to him a third time, 'Simon son of John, do you love me?' Peter was upset that he asked him the third time, 'Do you love me?' and said, 'Lord, you know everything; you know I love you'. Jesus said to him, 'Feed my sheep'. (*Jn* 21:15-17)

St Basil

Death held sway until Christ died. The grave was bitter and our prison indestructible until the Shepherd went down and brought to His sheep confined there the good news of their release. He gave them a pledge of their resurrection and called them to a new life beyond the grave.

St Augustine

Our Lord asked Peter who had denied Him three times for a threefold declaration of love. Christ had been raised to life in the flesh, and Peter to life in the Spirit, because when Christ died from the torments He had endured, Peter also died as a result of denying his Master. Christ the Lord who was raised from the dead, raised up Peter through the Apostle's love for Him. Having obtained the assurance of that love, He entrusted His Sheep to Peter's care.

St John Fisher

'Now this is eternal life: that they may know you, the only true God and Jesus Christ whom you have sent.' Here is even learning enough for me to my life's end.

Blessed Teresa of Calcutta

God is the friend of silence because He is not found in noise and restlessness. The essential thing is not what we say, but what God says to us and through us. Jesus always waits for us in silence, and in this silence He speaks to us. He will speak to our soul and there we will hear His voice.

Catechism of the Catholic Church

Peter's appointment and commission are inherited by his successors who are the Popes and Christ's vicars on earth and the pastoral office, with royal authority and responsibility, is at the heart of the Church and is perpetuated by the bishops under the primacy of the Pope (no.881)

Prayer

Heavenly Father, you sent your Son Jesus as Good Shepherd. Give us the grace to recognise the voice of the Shepherd and respond with fidelity.

Our Father, Hail Mary, Glory be to the Father etc.

11. The risen Lord entrusts to his disciples the mission to the world

V. We adore you Lord and praise you

R. Because by your death and resurrection
   you give life to the world

Reading from Holy Scripture

Meanwhile the eleven disciples set out for Galilee, to the mountain where Jesus had arranged to meet them. When they saw him they fell down before him, though some hesitated. Jesus came up and spoke to them. He said, 'All authority in heaven and on earth has been given to me. Go, therefore, make disciples of all the nations; baptise them in the name of the Father and of the Son and of the Holy Spirit, and teach them to observe all the commands I gave you. And know that I am with you always; yes, to the end of time.' (*Mt* 28:16-20)

St Bonaventure

Our first resurrection begins with our obedience to God, and is completed by our perseverance in doing His will. If we continue in obedience as long as we live, our second resurrection begins and we shall abide in a glory that knows no end.

St Teresa of Avila

Peter and the Apostles are the supreme examples of evangelisation, their achievements all the more remarkable and heaven-blessed in that they did not see the full results of their efforts and the fulfilment of Our Lord's promises.

St Therese of Lisieux

My mission is to make others love God as I love Him, to give to souls my little way of trust and self-surrender.

St Edmund Campion

Almighty God, send us your grace and set us at accord before the day of payment.

Prayer

Dear Lord, I will try to find a lift by which I may be raised to you, for I am too small to climb the steep stairway to perfection. (*St Therese of Lisieux*)

Our Father, Hail Mary, Glory be to the Father etc.

12. The risen Lord ascends to the Father

V. We adore you Lord and praise you

R. Because by your death and resurrection
you give life to the world

Reading from Holy Scripture

They asked 'Lord, has the time come? Are you going to restore the kingdom to Israel?' He replied, 'It is not for you to know times or dates that the Father has decided by his own authority, but you will receive power when the Holy Spirit comes on you, and then you will be my witnesses…indeed to the ends of the earth'. As he said this he was lifted up while they looked on, and a cloud took him from their sight…suddenly two men in white were standing near them and they said, 'Why are you men from Galilee standing here looking into the sky? Jesus who has been taken up from you into heaven, this same Jesus will come back in the same way as you have seen him go there.'(*Ac* 1:6-11)

St Leo the Great

We are blessed because Our Lord, having provided for everything concerning the preaching of the Gospel and the mysteries of the New Covenant, went up to Heaven before the eyes of the disciples. Our Redeemer's visible presence has passed into the Sacraments. Our faith is nobler and stronger because sight has been replaced by doctrine whose authority is accepted by believing hearts that are enlightened from on high.

Blessed John XXIII

The Lord's Ascension and final return to His father is the fulfilment of His promises, a surety for all to whom He has promised to prepare a place in Heaven and be with the Trinity for ever. He encourages us not to be hampered by temporal concerns but to trust the will of God that draws us heavenward.

St Teresa Benedicta of the Cross

Our Lord remains present in the Tabernacle, not for His own sake but for ours. It is His delight to be with 'the children of men'. He understands what we are and our need for His personal nearness.

St John Fisher

Lord,...clothed with the new garment of immortality, you entered the Holy of Holies that is Heaven. Before the throne of your heavenly Father, you show the Blood of great price that you have poured out for all sinners. This sacrifice is so pleasing and acceptable to God that He cannot but take pity on us, and show mercy to all who are truly repentant.

Prayer

Father in Heaven, our minds were prepared for the coming of your Kingdom when you took Christ beyond our sight so that we might seek Him in His glory. May we follow where He has led and find our hope in His glory.

Our Father, Hail Mary, Glory be to the Father etc.

13. Waiting for the Holy Spirit with Mary the mother of Jesus

V. We adore you Lord and praise you

R. Because by your death and resurrection
   you give life to the world

Reading from Holy Scripture

So from the Mount of Olives...they went back to Jerusalem,...and when they reached the city they went to the upper room where they were staying; there were Peter and John, James and Andrew, Philip and Thomas, Bartholomew and Matthew, James son of Alphaeus and Simon the Zealot, and Jude son of James. All these joined in continuous prayer, together with several women, including Mary the mother of Jesus. (*Ac* 1:12-14)

St Irenaeus

Just as Jesus was commissioned and sent by the Father so, when He returned to Heaven, the Spirit proceeded from the Father and the Son.

St Mary Magdalene of Pazzi

Come Holy Spirit, may the unison of the Father and the will of the Son come to us. Spirit of Truth, you are the reward of the Saints, the refreshment of souls, light in darkness, the riches of the poor, the treasury of lovers, the satisfaction of the hungry, the consolation of the pilgrim Church. You descended to Mary and the Word was made flesh. Bring about in us by grace what you accomplished in her by grace and nature.

Second Vatican Council

The Spirit dwells in the Church and in the hearts of the faithful as in a temple. He guides her into all truth, unites her in communion and service, bestows His gifts, and adorns her with the fruits of His grace. By the power of the Gospel, He allows her to keep the freshness of youth and leads her to perfect union with her Spouse. The Spirit and the Spouse both say to the Lord Jesus, 'Come!'

John Paul II

The Mother of the Risen Saviour was with the disciples in the Upper Room, awaiting the descent of the Holy Spirit and witnessing the birth of the Church on the day of Pentecost.

Prayer

Mary, you prayed with the Apostles in the Upper Room as you waited for the coming of the Holy Spirit. Ask for His renewed outpouring on all men and women so that they will respond to their vocation and mission in life as branches of the True Vine called to bear fruit in the life of the world. Mother of humanity, pray for us 'now and at the hour of our death.' (*John Paul II*)

Our Father, Hail Mary, Glory be to the Father etc.

14. The risen Lord sends the Spirit promised to the disciples

V. We adore you Lord and praise you

R. Because by your death and resurrection
you give life to the world

Reading from Holy Scripture

When Pentecost day came round, they had all met in one room, when suddenly they heard what sounded like a powerful wind from heaven, the noise of which filled the entire house in which they were sitting; and something appeared to them that seemed like tongues of fire; these separated and came to rest on the head of each of them. They were all filled with the Holy Spirit, and began to speak foreign languages as the Spirit gave them the gift of speech. (*Ac* 2:1-6)

St Irenaeus

St Luke says that after the Ascension, the Spirit came down on the disciple at Pentecost with power to grant all nations entry into life, and to open a new testament. And so, in every language, they sang a hymn to God in unison; for the Spirit brought the scattered races together in a unity, and offered to the Father the first fruits of all the nations.

St Leo the Great

The clarion call of the Gospel has rung out, and a rain of charismatic gifts, a river of blessings waters every dry land, for 'the Spirit of God sweeps over the waters to renew the face of the earth,' and a blaze of new light dispels our former darkness.

Blessed John XXIII

At the Last Supper in the Upper Room, Our Lord promised the Apostles the Holy Spirit, and it was in that very same room, in the presence of His Mother, they received Him as God's supreme gift. He is the consoler and giver of life to all men and women, and is continually within the Church throughout the ages. The Church's triumphs are not always visible but they are always there.

Benedict XVI

Pentecost is the birth of the Church through the working of the Holy Spirit... The Spirit enters a holy community at prayer in union with Mary and the Apostles: a Church One, Holy, Apostolic. It is also Catholic because the Holy Spirit, divine love, shows His presence in the gift of tongues that enables a universal understanding, a unity in diversity.

Prayer

Lord, let your gaze penetrate our hearts and illuminate the direction that our lives should take. On the day of Pentecost, you stirred the hearts of those who had clamoured for your death on Good Friday and brought them to conversion. In this way, you give hope to all. (*Benedict XVI*)

Our Father, Hail Mary, Glory be to the Father etc.

Concluding prayer

Father, around your throne the Saints, our brothers and sisters, sing your praise forever. Their glory fills us with joy, and their communion with us in the Church gives us inspiration and strength as we hasten on our pilgrimage of faith, eager to meet them.